*Other titles*
*by*
*Corey Hamilton*

**Keep Left**
**Society's Grip**
**Exit Is A Safe Place**
**No One Shall Be Spared**
**Open Up**
**Mash Notes**
**Too Personal**
**Lonely Night Songs**
**2 Days**
**Unhyped**
**Time Marches On**
**Thirty Three**
**VI**
**What If?**
**Magic Bus**
**How I Remember It**
**Cease & Desist**
**Sensible Shoes**
**Do Not Ever Have Any Good Ideas**
**DNA**
**I Am NOT With The Band**
**Wedge Politics**
**My Side Project**

# Mash Notes:
# Volume 2

Copyright © 2005 Corey Hamilton

All rights reserved. No part of this book may be reproduced or transmitted in any form or by any means, graphic, mechanical or electronic, including photocopying and recording, or by any information storage or retrieval system without written permission from the publisher, except for brief passages quoted in review.

Library and Archives Canada Cataloguing in Publication

Hamilton, Coery, 1971-
    Mash notes vol. 2/ Corey Hamilton.

Poems and prose.
ISBN 978-0-9697305-1-4 (v. 2)

    I. Title.

PS8565.A5347M38 2008        C811'.54        C2007-906816-2

Front cover photograph by Corey Hamilton © 2005
Back cover photograph of author by Randall Edwards © 2008
www.redwardsphoto.com
Design/layout by Corey Hamilton

*First Printing*

Published by Dramatic Situations
          P.O. Box 696
          Edmonton, AB
          T5J 2L4
          CANADA
www.dramaticsituations.com

# Mash Notes: Volume 2

Corey Hamilton

-masculine n 1: a male person 2: a noun, pronoun, adjective, or inflectional form or class of the masculine gender 3: the masculine gender
mas·cu·lin·ize \'mas-kyə-lə-ˌnīz\ vt -ized; -iz·ing : to give a predominantly masculine character to; esp : to cause (a female) to take on male characteristics
ma·ser \'mā-zər\ n [microwave amplification by stimulated emission of radiation] : a device that utilizes the natural oscillations of atoms or molecules between energy levels for generating electromagnetic radiation in the microwave region of the spectrum
¹mash \'mash\ n [ME, fr. OE *māx-*; akin to MHG *meisch* mash] 1: crushed malt or grain meal steeped and stirred in hot water to ferment (as for the production of beer or whiskey) 2: a mixture of ground feeds for livestock 3: a soft pulpy mass
²mash vt 1 *CRUSH, SMASH* <~ a finger> 2: to subject (as crushed malt) to the action of water with heating and stirring in preparing wort
³mash vt [prob. fr. ²mash] : to flirt with or seek to gain the affection of
⁴mash n : *CRUSH* 3
MASH *abbr* mobile army surgical hospital
¹mash·er \'mash-ər\ n : one that mashes <a potato ~>
²masher n : a man who makes passes at women
¹mask \'mask\ n [MF *masque*, fr. OIt *maschera*] 1 a (1) : a cover or partial cover for the face used for disguise (2) : a person wearing a mask : MASKER b (1) : a figure of a head worn on the stage in antiquity to identify the character and project the voice (2) : a grotesque false face worn at carnivals or in rituals c : an often grotesque carved head or face used as an ornament (as on a keystone) d : a sculptured face or a copy of a face made by means

# F.Y.I.

The poetry in this book was taken from my two most recent (at the time this book was written/compiled/June 2005) notebooks. An explanation for the short story "Chef's Salad" can be found on page 90 of this book.

Thanks.

#1078

It's always a lay-away plan
When I go out on my own
And I try to meet someone new

## HELPLESS PARENTS

The past hunts me down
Like a hunter seeks out
His already wounded prey
I wrote you
She made it
So that's why I washed
All of my books last night
Because she made it
That I was at
The bottom of the food chain
I wrote you
And now you never notice me
When I noticed your beauty
I should have looked
The other way
Because my silhouette
Was destroyed by your smile
The other night
I dreamt
That my father
Put a gun to my head
And pulled the trigger
The gun was all but empty
And when the one and only bullet
Was fired
He turned the gun slightly away
So that all I felt
Was powder burns
And the bullet's breath
As it left its chamber
When she passed by
I was just as useless
As the parent
Who feels that they are helpless
To control their child
If you can't control your life
Then how can you control

Your offspring's
You have to live long
Or live loud
You can't do both
Because you'll lose your voice
Eventually
And then it is an automatic
Breakdown after the loud
Has gone away
Live long or
Live loud
I choose the latter
Why is it that
I never get a chance to
Say no to
The people I want to
Say no to
And never get to
Say yes to
The people I want to
Say yes to
I had a dream this morning
All artists
Whether they were sell outs or not
Poets or painters
Photographers or sculptors
Musicians or even chefs
Were being arrested
And put in jail
I thought about you this evening
And how your old and cold image
Destroys your current state
Why be something you are not
Especially when it has no benefit
I have lived loud
And now
My past is catching up
To my future

## PUBLIC TRANSPORTATION

I take the bus
Everywhere I go
And contrary to popular belief
Of the city that runs it
It is not fun
And it is not always convenient or easy
It's a shuttle of despair and heartbreak
Most days
With a bit of people
Who are too cool to be there
So they look through you
And prefer to stand
Rather than sitting next to someone
When you need to be with someone
And the freaks who prefer to sit next to you
When you need to be alone
What about the drunk teenage girls
Who talk loudly
Of who they sucked off that night
The loud drunks
The loud cellphones
The loud walkmans
The loud perfumes
The loud clothes
And the loud talk
It's midnight and I have to put up with
Their swearing and bragging
The bus driver yells to keep it down
Another time
Getting on the bus
The driver leaves before
Everyone is on the bus
Saying if you're not here now
Too bad
It's too bad
About all of the winter mornings
On the bus

That kill your happiness
As soon as you step on
With your exact change
I can smell the desperation
Of all the people
Wishing that they could get out of here
And just get a good paying job
To buy a car or
Get close to home
Or to get all of the above
But we all get stuck in traffic
Because other cars won't let us in
I wish that I could afford a car
I need that independence again
But I am too scatter-brained to drive
Maybe there is someone else like me
I could talk to on this lonely caravan
Maybe there's a female my age
And we could take the bus together
And turn this desperately lonely public transit
Into private transit
To forget that loud foreign blathering
To miss the drunks all together
Private transit
I take the bus and it's public torture
I want to change it
Into private transit
Just for two who don't need to shout
Or stare at emptiness
Just stare at each other
And make it
Private transit

#1081

## ENVY

Every time I see a very expensive vehicle
I think of that Janis Joplin song

*O Lord won't you buy me a Mercedes Benz*
*My friends all drive Porches, I must make amends*

If you have an auto that expensive
More likely than not
You can afford the upkeep

*Worked hard all my lifetime*
*No help from my friends*

I've gotten here with a little help
From my parents
But mostly on my own
And when I see the wealth
I know what envy means
Not jealousy but envy

*O Lord won't you buy me a colour t.v.*
*Dialing for dollars is trying to find me*

And when I see all that wealth
I think that some of it
Was meant for me
I mean
There must be enough to go around

*I wait for delivery*
*Each day until 3*

How long do I work?
How long do I wait?
Until I get my break
Just one good bright break
And I know I can

*O Lord won't you buy me a night on the town*
*I'm counting on you Lord please don't let me down*

Every once in awhile
I go out with my friends
And see them struggling to get through the evening
Without worrying about their bills
Just like me

*Prove that you love me*
*And buy the next round*

I wish that I could walk into a bar
And buy everyone I know
The next round
Because if there is a "Lord"
He's too busy for me
And my friends
But that's okay
For we have our problems
But we are getting by
But I am getting by
It's just the envy in my guts
That's getting to me

## A PROMISE OF GUILT

It's all retro-active
When you don't look at me
When we talk
This causes me
To want to slip
In and out of consciousness
And write "write" like this
Until my arm decomposes
With the rest of me
I want to die
And then get some payment
For my art
Because isn't that the way
It's supposed to happen
Hopefully the payment
Would be retro-active
To compensate me
For all of the types of pain
I have endured
Self-inflicted or otherwise
This could go on for a long time
But it never does
Retro-active is a short trade
And so is your talk
When you don't look at me

## NOVEMBER 12, 2001

I wish it was now
I wish a good change
Would come now
I hope for a better time
I hope for a wish
To come true
I pray for it to end
I pray that my hope
Opens up and blossoms
Would you stand beside me
Even though I am a sad soul
Even though we aren't friends
Acquaintance is not enough
I need more calls
I need more arms to hold me
I need more hopes and wishes
To come true
I wish someone would understand
I hope someone understands
I don't normally pray
But I will make an exception
I pray a change comes before
My final dance ends
For it should be a dance
That lasts longer than 30 years

#1089

The moon was just like the sun
On the night that we put her down
Blazing red like it was the end of the world
We had to cut her up
And leave her for the vultures
Because the drugs were destroying
Her beautiful body and free mind
Like an aggressive wrecking crew

## CALL ME AN ACQUAINTANCE

I went to the trouble
Of trying to find your phone number
But to no avail
I thought that I would find out
If time heals all wounds
If we talked
I haven't heard from you in years
And I guess that's the way
It will stand
None of my friends have called me
In weeks
So I thought I would see how long
I could hold out not calling them
It's been about the same length of time
The phone has been silent
And I guess that's the way
It will stand
Until either myself or you buckles
I am hoping that it will be you
Then I can say "It's been awhile"
And then I can ask
If we are really friends
Or just acquaintances
Because it has been so long
Since we last talked
Since we last went out
Since we last looked in each other's eyes
Are we friends
If we don't converse on a regular basis?
Don't call me friend
If I have to write
A finger pointing poem about you
Don't call me friend if
We never meet up or talk
Call me an acquaintance
And I would feel much better
About this silent phone

On this lonely evening

#1097

Never apologize
For something you created
Never ever apologize
For something that you have created

#1098

## ILLUSION OF HOPE

It's just an illusion
Of wealth
It's just a parody
Of happiness
What happens when
You realize
You have nothing to offer
Anyone else
But your insecurities
Your delusions
Your loneliness
Is that all you get
When you befriend me?
No
It's not so
This is just the way I am
When I am alone
With my real friends
Books and music and art and write
And
And
And
Maybe I should take
Another pill
To make it all go away
Turn this all
Into an illusion
An illusion of hope

#1102

## NOBODY IS ON MY GUEST LIST

I made a 4 month old baby
Giggle with glee
It made me so happy
To make someone's day
No matter the age
It made me happy
So I told you that
I made a baby smile up a storm
And your single 40 plus year old
Typical bitter woman's response was,
"She (the baby) will grow up
And learn not to smile at you"
I wanted to ask
What that meant
I wanted to say
"It's comments like that
That keep you single at your age"
But I didn't say a word
I just walked away
Feeling like I don't belong there

I had a dream about you
The other night
I was wearing an expensive suit
And I had bought you
A red silk dress
With spaghetti straps
It clung to your youthful body
Like a second layer of skin
You looked beautiful
I woke up excited
That I had had a dream about you
And I eventually realized that
You hadn't called me in months
And I haven't seen you
Even longer than that
And you never wear dresses

You said that our relationship
Wouldn't change
Even though you moved away
The relationship did change
And it left me feeling lonelier than ever

This is why
These are some of the reasons why
And you are why
Nobody is on my guest list

## IN RAGE

They are all strangers
To me
To me
They are all unknown
Waiting for calls
Calling and too busy
And never returning
What do you do
When you are surrounded
By people who you only know
By their names
You ask yourself questions like
Who am I to be so shy?
What did I do wrong?
When will it begin?
When will they see me?
Why can't I relate?
How come they don't come to me?
Who are they not to think of me?
The questions are pragmatic
The answers won't lie
Maybe that's why I get tattoos and shave my head
Maybe that's why I listen to my music loud
Maybe that's why I read so much
Maybe that's why I stay inside so much
Maybe that's why
They are all strangers
To me
My lover
A book I wrote years ago
My best friend
A painting I did a few months ago
A new friend
This poem I just met
Narcissism
In the absence of love
Is that even possible?

It must be
Because I am still alive
I know who I am
You don't know who I am
And you don't seem
To want to make any effort
To see me
So if that's the way it will be
That's the way it will be
It had to come to this
I look at my art
And know that they are not
Strangers to me
And you all are

## BUILDINGS

It's quiet architecture
Buildings that are new
But abandoned
That I latch on to
Like a leach to a bare leg
The emptiness
I can relate to sometimes
It's too much of not enough
I thought I heard someone say
There are a hell of a lot of questions
Sometimes when something so big
Can be so empty
How can the same mistakes be made
Over and over again and again
I ask myself out loud
Especially big ones
Sometimes it's so hard
To remember all that's been done
Right or wrong
Weak or strong
It's quiet architecture
The buildings with only a few
Occupants of loneliness
The few lights on at night
Are almost pornographic
Like I shouldn't be looking at
A few lighted windows
When all else is dark
But there is always hope
When there is a little light
Showing through the darkness

#1108

## WOMAN'S' WORK

It's never done
Until a period of silence ends it
She responded in pain
When I came within a foot of her
I said
I would stop and that
It wasn't like I was touching her
In her swimsuit area
She turned to me
With spittle flying
And a voice of rage
Saying
That that was sexual harassment
That period
Ended it for me
Not wanting to get any closer
For fear of stepping over
The line again or
A line again
I thought she warranted me
To do some sharing for once
I thought she warranted me
Being nice to her
But a period ended it
And I see saw see saw
I should treat her no different
Than a stranger
On the street
That I care not to know
It's never done

It's never done
Days later
I was washing my dishes
And she surprised me
I didn't see her or it coming
She was dressed smartly

While saying that she was looking for me
Ten seconds of silence
I said that I had just finished eating
Ten seconds of silence
She said that it was nice to meet me
Ten seconds of silence
I said same here
Ten seconds of silence
She said that she hoped everything worked out for me
Ten seconds of silence
I said that I hoped everything worked out for her
Ten seconds of silence
She said see you later
Ten seconds of silence
I said later skater
And that was that
She smiled and looked me in the eyes
During those seventy seconds of silence
Like I was supposed to say more
Than what was said
But after you are accused of guilt
When you bleed nothing but innocence
The silence is a period that ends it even when
It's never done

It's never done
Until a period ends it
There was a strange dichotomy
Going on there
The silence said
So much more
Than the spoken words
After being the accused
I would no longer
Feed her
She would have to bleed on her own
A period of words ended it
A period of silence confirmed it
And a period of time proves it
No sharing was meant to be
Between her and myself
I would pass on her

Knowing full well
That the punctuation of silence
Was full of contradiction
And I realize that
She's not worth it
Because there's plenty more
Fish in the sea like her
And I know that
A woman's' work is never done
Until a period ends it
And another woman
And another period
Ends it

## DREAM FLOWER

I had a dream about a flower
Last night
The flower was big and flush with lush petals
That were magenta, purple and red
The colors melted into one another
So the flower looked as if
It glowed
So I will wait for it
Like waiting for a drug to take effect
And when the feeling comes
I will do a painting of it
To justify my obsession
With this dream
I keep hoping
That every time I sleep
I will see that flower again
And I would wake up again
With all of the same feelings again
So when times of sadness swarm over me
I can think of the flower
Fresh in my mind
And it will take me from the ugly
I see
To the beautiful
I need to see
I had a dream about a flower
Last night
And I awoke from the dream
With a gentle smile on my face

## THE CHASE

The more people I meet
The more I like myself
The middle of a long cold winter
I know how cold it is
Just opening my eyes
For the first time in the morning
I am supposed to chase you
But I got tired of that game
Because I am too old
For all that running
So I call everyone I know
To talk to someone
And no one is home
I am the only one
In the universe
With free time on their hands
I cannot swim anymore
Because I concentrate too much
On trying to convince myself
I am not alone
But when I meet people
I am almost always let down
So the more people I meet
The more I like myself

## MAKING THE NEW DRAMA TEACHER HAPPY

I am afraid of fuel
Because it might bring about
My swan song quicker
Once I get out of debt
You will all be sorry
Some days I want more
Other days I am okay
With what I have got
I am sometimes excited
And other times I am bored
But what do you expect
When you are as lonely as
An unbought postcard
Sitting dusty on a rack
In a dusty small town store
It may be so bad
That it will never be the same
But that's the difference
Between getting stale
And staying fresh
When you got something
To keep you on edge
Maybe I will stop taking
My medication
And move to the coast
And never be heard from again
Now <u>that's</u> fuel
Now <u>that's</u> something to not be afraid of
A big change
And forgetting about my swan song

#1120

## LATE FRIDAY AND EARLY SATURDAY

Here's how it usually goes:
Watch a bit of television
Listen to a lot of music
This time was a little different
I did a painting of "a touch"
Two hands gently touching each other
The way lovers' hands would
On a hot summers' day
Walking in a park
I miss that sort of bonding moment
I miss those sort of bonding moments
But with my music and art
I miss it less
And this time around
I feel okay

## NO CHIP HERE

I wear my blood on my sleeve and collar
And I keep my heart in my hands
Held tightly behind my back
I am not sure why I do this
Because I would rather
Be shot in the heart
Than in the head
I wear all this blood
Because it says to all
What I am
I would rather be open
With my head than my heart
And now my blood comes from my head
And goes to my heart secondary
I try to use my head
But sometimes my heart
But most times my heart
Gets in the way
I am wearing a white suit
Covered in my blood
With my head intact
And my heart
Behind my back

#1122

      The dream is always the same. I am in a school and I am late for an exam. I am panicking because I have forgotten where my locker is. So I go to the main office to find out where it is. I am in a hurry and time is of the essence. I get to my locker and I have realized that I have forgotten the combination to my lock on my locker door. So I can't get it open and I have to go to the main office again to get the combination. I hurry back and get my locker open and all of my stuff I need out and rush to the testing room. I am late but they let me in. Now I panic even more because I have forgotten everything I need to know to pass the exam.

## PORTICO

I won't go to your church
Because the gates are not wide open
He was on the other side of the street
And you made like he wasn't special
When we are all special
She walked with Buddhist Monks
And you discarded her beliefs
Because it wasn't your truth
And maybe you are with me
Because it will make you feel better
About yourself
If you convert a lost soul
I've had enough
About yourself
When it's hot outside
You won't acknowledge
The liars and the thief
And when it's cold outside
You are slumming with the beggars
Because it makes you feel better
About yourself
One more steamed milk
Helps you ignore the blade of the knife
That we have all lied and thieved
Because in one way or another
We have all been prostitutes
To get our own way
Have you ever been to a job interview?
Or on a stage?
Or begged for quarters in the cold?
Then you should know what I mean
We can be friends
If I call you for your truth
But I don't like a truth
That has clauses to exclude
Visible minorities as well as others
With ways of life that you don't agree with

Go by your book
Go buy your book
And I will write my own
There is no manual for life
But that's where we part our ways
You follow your path
That narrow for only one
And I'll walk down mine
With all the ones your book
Doesn't approve of
They are the true friends of mine
Because they aren't judgmental
Of what makes me wander
This is a journal entry for Christmas
For you
This is a journal entry for a beautiful winter's day
For me

## MUSIC TO MY EARS

The night found me
With the dim lights on
Reading by myself
And only minding the scenario
A little bit

The day found me
With no socks on my feet
Reading by myself
Not minding it
One little bit

The night bites into me
Like a hyena
The day is like
A beak of a woodpecker
Tap tapping away
On a tree

Music to my ears

God doesn't laugh at my jokes
But I won't sacrifice myself
Because of it
I move on knowing that
Last weekend was just a moment of weakness

The more I read to myself
The more I play to myself
The more I play with myself
The more I listen by myself
The more I like myself

I don't want it
And more importantly
I don't need it
To get by

I find it all in myself

The more people I meet
The more I like myself
And that's
Music to my ears

## THIS AND THAT

It's darker than
A little of this
It's lighter than
Most of that
It's when the sun
Streams through my blinds
At the break of dawn
And even the crows
Caw cawing sound marvelous
I hear young children running
And laughing
Just outside my open window
The children try to keep up with
The light cool breeze
Just outside my open window
It's more of a complete day
Than that of a work day
It's less of a bad day
Than my darkest day hour
It's looking at my sun faded
26 year old Curious George doll
And thinking of all of the memories
That linger in his smile
It's looking at a sky
In an Alex Colville painting
It's reading "The Fountainhead"
By Ayn Rand
It's listening to Crazy Horse's
Self titled first album
It's all of this and more
When it's a warm summer afternoon
At a diamond
Smelling hot dogs
Watching all of the people
And the game
And all of that
It was sometimes darker

Now it's lighter
More or less
From this and that
More or less
Of this and that

#1143

## OBJECTIONAL ACTS OF ROMANCE

I am glad
It worked out the way it did
Because it serves you right to suffer
You and I
Went into an adult movie store
And the protesters
Weren't protesting the store
They were protesting
Us going into the store
With our love
Or what little was left
Of our love
Because it's easy
To read in a different language
In front of a crowd
That doesn't know that language
I owe you nothing
Not even a sleepless night
Move and nobody gets hurt
Because I am happy
The way it worked out

## SPAM

Once the dope wears off
And the last bit of adrenaline
Dies out
It makes me realize
That this big new bed
Is lonelier
Than the old small bed
So I get up
And go to my computer
To check my e-mail
And all that's there is porn
And Russian women
Wanting to marry western men
Figures
At a low point
And I get porn
And desperate Russian women
Desperately trying to get out of
Their homeland
This makes me feel
More desperate and
More lonely
So I leave the front cover
Of Bob Dylan's "Nashville Skyline"
Lp out in plain view
Because it's such a happy cover
The dope has worn off
And Russian women
And Bob Dylan
Don't help

#1160

I want to have sex with you
In my room
In the middle of the afternoon
With the bright sunshine
Trying to come through
The drawn blinds
So we can see all of our faults
Clearly
And then
The next day
Call it "making love"
Under my breath

## TRADE OFF

Give me your cancer
And I will slip away
With my unused potential
And you could go on being
Successful at what you do
Have you taken your last drag
Of your last cigarette?
I suppose you have
Is it too late though
To give me your cancer
To cure my current dismal view
Of my current dismal world
I have seen enough
Too much in fact
So is it too late
To give me your cancer?
So you can go on
Your skiing trips in the winter
And your golf games in the summer
Give me your cancer
So you can make your last payment
On your new home and business
And then retire
To your skiing trips in the winter
And your golf games in the summer
And the odd artistic endeavor
That you may have at any given moment
Turn _your_ cancer into _my_ cancer
And it would cure
What goes wrong in my brain
Eventually
And then I could feel
Like I've given back
All that you gave to me
Not as an insult
Just so we could say that
"We are even"

And we could then meet
At some time and somewhere else
And start all over again
With a clean slate

## TAKEN

I am in love with your girlfriend
She is so young and beautiful
Bright and sharp
And so young
But I said that already
Don't worry
I won't steal her from you
I love her image
I don't want to know about
Or deal with
Her P.M.S. or streak marks
In her underwear
I just want to love her image
And let you handle
Her extra baggage
And I'll just put her on a pedestal
And let my imagination
Do all of the work
And fall in love again tomorrow
With another
Young and beautiful girlfriend

#1163

I gently caress your face
With the back of my right hand
Against your left side
You smiled gently almost
Embarrassed at this sign of affection
In public
I stopp and we continue
Eating our respective meals
In our respective seats
Quietly listening
To the quiet noise
In this small quiet restaurant
On this sunny afternoon

This is pure fiction
I dreamt it last night

#1165

## MANIPULATIVE

All stoned up on tranquilizers
Hoping that you call
Wondering what I would say
Totally numb
From the last few weeks
I hope that you call now
Because it is so nice to hear your voice
Calm and pleasantly reassuring

All stoned up on tranquilizers
Hoping that if you call
My intense depression
Doesn't scare you off
And make you want to
Forget all about me
Hoping to hear your voice
So its reassuring pleasant calmness
Eases my inner demons

#1168

Something ventured
Nothing gained
The story of my life
So far

#1175

## NOBODY LIVES LIKE ME

I wake up early
Long before even the ants
I wake up early
Just to pay the rent
Just to pay the rent?!
Hardly
I wake up early
So the days
The long days
Melt into one long season
And then I take a bunch of pills
And then go back to sleep early
And sleep my troubles away
Underneath a prairie sky
But over top of my city nightmares
I will leave this open
Until I finish it all
So I can rest my bed head head bed
And listen to these writings
Until I finish it all
In the express lane
Of my small home
Hoping that I will out grow
The express lane
Of my small home
And grow into
A bumper to bumper traffic jam
Of a mansion
That's why I wake so early
To remember where I am
And to see where I am going

## OUT OF ANGER

I fumble with my keys
Out of anger
Because she said that we were "friends"
Yet I hadn't talked to her
In over a year
A lot happens in one whole year
Four seasons
A couple of lucky Friday the 13ths
And some other more memorable things
But she never thought to call
Or return my calls
Or bite through my thin skin
Or to see my ups and downs
Or even past promises made by her
Never to come true for me
In every action
There is an opposite and equal reaction
She left me with her action
And she left me feeling
I was the opposite reaction
But not the equal

I still haven't been able to get
My damn keys
In the fucking key hole
And now
I am all out of anger

#1178

## ON THEM

He said that
He wears his past
Like an overcoat
No matter how hot
No matter how cold
I feel like hugging him
And telling him
That we all wear our pasts
Like a coat
I can relate to him
But on a much smaller scale

Bernard Shakey
Henry Chinaski
RRose Selavy
Jack Frost
Wayne Milton
Hang your overcoat
On them
Keep it up
You may not be able to
But they are willing and able
To take it
Maybe I am naive
To feel this way

I wonder
Along with you
Whom those bells are ringing for
They are ringing for you
They are honoring you
And your fortitude
And your commitment to your work
And your perseverance

You could always lose
A little more

He lives large
And would have
A lot more to lose
Than someone like myself
Who has to live small
I wonder if he realizes
That it seems as if
His complaint
Could be made
By anyone
But that if he was
Small like me
It wouldn't have had
The impact on me
That his large overcoat did

Maybe when you are big
Maybe when you are big
Maybe when you are small
Maybe when you are small
Large or small
We all wear our pasts
Positive or negative
Like an overcoat
White or black
Black or white
Maybe I am just naive

If you can remember
What you came to escape from
And you are able to sleep well
Then that's all that counts
That is all that counts

Maybe I am just naive

#1179

## WHERE'S MY FUCKING MONEY YOU OWE ME?

I won't compromise
Compare me to whoever you want
It doesn't matter
Because I started my work
Long before my senses kicked in
I wouldn't recommend anyone else
To go this route though
Because it takes a lot longer
To find yourself in your work
To find your work in yourself
People talk to me
About this painter
About that writer
About this photographer
About that style
And I can't relate
I live in a small bubble
I am very insulated
From what I see as distractions
Others see as inspirations
I am scared to fall off of my path
Because it has worked
For me
So well
Maybe not financially
But on another level
It works for me
But I feel no one can understand
This level
Keeps me going
And at other times
It seems like an anvil
Tied around my neck

## AMERICAN WAR

This is the stink
Of the apple pie you just puked up
This is the stink
Of what you thought you conquered
The sand and hot wind
That blows
Stings your already sunburnt flesh
Write home
When the next car bomb goes off asshole
Your most reliable news resource
Is a bunch of candy coated racists
And wouldn't dare interview
Ken Jarecke
From the last time around
You know what?
There will never be
A world without tears
When a war on nothing
Gets better television ratings
Than the Superbowl or the World Series
Death is the way
The only way out
To be reprogrammed
Follow the cult's orders
And death for <u>you</u> is the only way
The only way out
You started it
You started this war on nothing
And they will finish it
This American War

#1184

## DON'T TELL ME TO CALM DOWN

The moment I wrote number one
It stabbed you in the heart
And left you in a bloody mess
On your kitchen floor
Because the moment I started
You finished
I don't care if you released
A dozen or more books since then

YOU ARE FINISHED

Something must be said about
Going on when you are not welcome anymore
So show me that you love me
And go to sleep
And never wake up
Ooooh
Did I provoke you?
Well that's my job shithead!
And just to set the record straight
I am into 65 year old women
As much as I am not into 18 year old girls
I am not

YOU ARE FINISHED

AND I AM NOT

#1190

## WHITE KNUCKLES, BARE ASSES

Late one night
We had passionate sex
For about three, three and a half hours
After we were finished
After a little chit chat
After a little bit of a rest
I went
And had a shower
By myself
After I was finished
I came out
And you were gone
No note
No nothing
Just gone
I quickly checked my apartment
A quick but extensive search
To make sure
Nothing was stolen
After I was sure
Nothing was stolen
I went back to bed
And fell into a peaceful sleep
Without a care
In the world

#1192

## FOOLS ON THE WHITE AVENUE

It was a good show
I had fun
The band played songs that
I recognized
And they played songs that
I didn't recognize
I waited for the bus after
The good show
Thinking that
The crowd was mostly drunk
And very young
I recognized six people there
Three of which
I didn't want to recognize
500 average is pretty good eh?
I am going home now
Dodging the staggering drunks
And other fools on the avenue
I apologize
For getting angry
For getting sullen
For going home early
And not wanting to play the game
Of looking good
Just to be looked at

It was a good show
I had fun
And it was
And it was
A momentary escape
From the kitten
Caught in the tree syndrome
Now I am home
Angry
Sullen
All in one

On an early night
Thinking of no one
But the band
That played well

#1194

## FOOD AND SUPPLIES

Did you have to do that?
Did you have to go and tell them?
What does it matter
If I go quietly
Or not?
They will never look at me
Like they did before
I will never forgive you
For how depressed
This will get me
I hope that you are happy
With this mess
Now I will never leave my home
Not even to get
Food and supplies
I will have my phone disconnected
Because it won't be needed anymore
For no one will call me anymore
Thanks a lot
I will shrivel up to a husk
And they
(You as well)
Won't find me till next spring
But that will be far too late
The second after you opened your mouth
And let the cat
Out of the bag
Was far too late
Thanks
Thanks a lot

#1297

## AS BEST I COULD

I lay alone in your bed
While you do your homework
I ask if you need a hand
Knowing full well
You have to do it on your own
Knowing full well
You would say, "no"
And you did
I fall in love with you
When you tell me
That you think you are
Falling in love with me
I knew full well
You were seeing someone else
And it all pushed me
To grip harder
And eventually
I gave up
And moved on
As best I could
And now every time I see you
You ignore me
And look the other way
I get the message
And move on
As best I can

#1298

## WARM CAR

I watched you
From inside your warm car
I watched you
Through the window  and rain
Kiss your boyfriend
On the lips
Right then
Blood ran and pumped
Into my head
And made my eyes
Match the weather outside

I knew I should have taken the bus home

**#1299**

As we watched the Northern Lights
I kissed you on the lips
You were more interested in the light show
At least I was still warm in my car with you

#1302

## LOOK HARDER

I see your disappointed eyes
And I know
I am just hanging on a limb
With my finger tips
The most important people
In my life
I seem to let down
All the time
Let's start again
And hopefully your stare
Won't pain me
But the most important people
In my life
Seem to let me down
All the time
Eye for an eye
Do you see my disappointed eyes?
No?
Well look harder
Look harder

#1306

## ASLEEP OR AWAKE

A little while ago
I woke up
And rolled over
To see the clock
Glaring exactly midnight
At me
I heard through the walls
People around me
Having all sorts of fun
My home
Is a piranha of sounds now
My bed is for me
To wrestle with myself in
And my skull
Is for me to wrestle
With myself in too
Asleep
Or awake
Sometimes I can't tell
Which I am
Maybe
I have to exercise more
Like my parents say
Lose some weight
Get healthy
By putting me in detention
And keeping it real
24/7
Telling people off
Who should be
And complimenting people
Who should be
And moving on
To the next challenge
And now I roll over
And read all of this
And I know what I have to do

Move on
Put my stuff out more
And move on
School is out
And I have graduated
With flying colors

this piece was written on
January 1st, 2005 at 1:40 am

## AGREED

He removed his toque
To show me
His freshly shaved head
The steam that rose
From his head
Melted together
With the smoke
From his joint
He took a drag
And told me
I was in a good position
And for once
I agreed with someone
Who said
I was in a good position
In life

#1319

## FOOLS BEING FOOLISH

I see people talking about
A lady down south
Who is in a vegetative state
And is slowly dying
They say she has a right to live
In her vegetative state
Her husband says
She didn't want this
Which contradicts the right to lifers
And her family
I will tell you this:
If it is the dead of winter
And it is minus thirty degrees
And I am in a vegetative state
Then roll me out into the cold
To freeze to death
Otherwise
Put a bullet in my head
I do <u>not</u> want to live that way
And not know that I am living
The right to lifers
Have good points
If you are a fool that is
The right to lifers
Are no different
Than the fools who bomb
Abortion clinics
Oh yeah,
I am pro-choice too

Fools.


this piece was written on March 25th, 2005

## TANIA VERSUS PATTI

I had a dream last night
That while I was sleeping
You sewed my eyes shut
With a needle and thread
All the while you wouldn't
Make me feel like I was the one
Even though my eyes were sewed shut
I could still see your insincere smile
Maybe it was all your youth could handle
But sometimes I don't buy into that
You won't take responsibility
For your actions
And neither will the president
Or your "then" friends
Good thing your family is rich
So you can get a good lawyer
Now you're on talk shows
Looking hot in your nice clothes
And long died hair
You're just like that girl
Who makes me feel bad
You make me feel bad
For believing that you were brain-washed
When I see how much control
You have on the talk shows
Good thing you were born into
A wealthy family
Or you really would have needed a gun
Tania versus Patti
Patti won
Unlike Tania and her 'friends'
Patti just watched for her own ass
And forgot Tania
And her friends
And she got you
Hook, line and sinker

#1325

## MESSAGE IN A BOTTLE

To whoever finds this
I love you
I have very little hope left
But what little I have
Hopes that someone
With a gentle soul finds this
So I can say
"I love someone"

I have had a lot of time
To write this out
And the one thing I have realized is
Love of one self
Can only go so far
Before the thread breaks
As kind as I am
Most don't see me that way

Nice guys finish last
And they don't get paid either
And the meek shall inherit the shit
And where has all of the time gone
And how alone do I have to feel
And last but not least
To whoever finds this
I love you

#621.3

## *"CHEF'S SALAD"*

This will seem dated. This will most likely seem dated almost immediately after you have finished reading it. It will probably be out of date even after you have finished turning this page. Regardless, I felt that I should write about this portion of my life, what was important that happened before, what's happening now and what may happen in the future. Again, it may seem dated.

It will seem dated probably because I was born and raised in a small town for 19 years of my life. The small town that I was born in is in Manitoba, just off of Highway 16 (or the Yellow Head). Highway 16 starts in British Columbia and goes all the way through Alberta, Saskatchewan and ends in Manitoba. If you have never been in a small town then you are missing out on tiny pieces of history. Everything in small towns is dated and everything that comes out of small towns is dated too, for if you go into a small town you will see styles that got burned up in a fury five years ago. You will see bake sales at the curling rink advertised in the cafes and post office. You will see trucks making u-turns in front of R.C.M.P. officers. You will hear cattle prices, hog prices, grain prices, alfalfa prices, canola prices and *Farmer's Almanac* weather prospects on the dusty radio waves. You will hear about Jim's son Sammy being scouted by the Toronto Blue Jays and then Sammy throwing his arm out weeks later. You will feel like you are in a Norman Rockwell painting from years ago. And then you realize that it is all dated. It's just that someone forgot to tell these pour souls that they are not needed anymore because the big cities have taken over, for better or for worse (sometimes I think that it is for worse but that is for another rant).

I realized all of this once I moved out into the big city that I was still dated, even though I am now 37. I still have this strong bond to the quiet peacefulness and surreal pastoral quality of small towns. I still need history and that is why I am rambling so.

I have been in several major (and several not so major) cities in Canada. Victoria, Vancouver, Kellowna, Kamloops, Jasper, Banff, Lake Louise, Edmonton, Red Deer, Calgary, Lethbridge, Drumheller, Lloydminster, Saskatoon, Regina, Brandon, Winnipeg, Thunderbay, Sudbury, Toronto, Ottawa, Hamilton, Montreal, Quebec City and all points in between. I have even seen several big cities in the U.S.A.. The big cities all reek of convenience, exhaust fumes, anger, hatred, fear, rape, violence, jet engines, drugs and money. I am practically deaf from all of the things that people take for granted in these "big" places. Every time I go for a walk I feel a million daggers slice my back open to the weathering processes, a grimy process that comes from people who are so small in their attitudes and their lifestyles that they need a life preserver every time they take a piss.

It is the same with almost everyone in these so called "big" cities, which to me resemble cold sores on a beautiful woman's mouth. Every one of these big cities are the same. I am not saying that small towns aren't, they are, but at least they don't have to struggle to grasp at their history as it slips away. Unfortunately, small towns *are* history. They don't have to fight for it. This I find touching. Touching because I can walk small town sidewalks and not have to watch my back or worry about some drugged up crazed blue collar worker going ballistic and spraying the street with bullets.

You may ask me why I then moved to a big city because it sounds as if I hate them and find nothing good about them. It's not true, I do like big cities and I do find some things good about them but I will get into this in more detail later on.

I go back to my birthplace to see my parents at the most twice a year. But no more because I start to feel like I am suffocating all over again. Then I go back to the city and I feel like I am being corroded away and I need a break so I go back to the small town I was born in again and it goes like this and has been going on like this for the past 18 years.

You probably want to know what I do for a living. I am a writer and have been a writer for as long as I can remember. I remember writing short stories when I was 10 or so and my parents saying things like, "what an active imagination," or, "he is so creative!" That all ended when I turned 16. That's when puberty was finishing and I was discovering girls and I was more confused about everything that I have ever been (or will be I imagine!). My writings got darker and what was thought to be imaginative and creative by my parents was reconstructed by them to be strange and silly. Their words changed to, "I don't understand," and "I don't like it," and better yet, "so what." (This is about the time that I discovered poetry, more on this later.). I could go on but it doesn't matter because it would only make me sound bitter. I will leave that up to my parents to be bitter, for I was supposed to take over the farm when I graduated from high school, but I didn't. I just got up and moved (more on this later too).

By this time I had turned 18 and I no longer gave a shit about what my parents or anyone else thought and this is why I moved. I saw a good portion of Canada and a bit of the U.S.. All along the way I wrote and did spoken word shows wherever I could. Cafes, book stores, bars even the odd street corner during a festival.

Finally in a big city someone heard me, this certain someone's job was to find new talent for a mid-sized publisher. This certain someone liked what I had to say and as the cliche goes, the rest is history. That was when I was 20. I settled in the big unnamed city and my first book came out when I was 21. I starved through a few more years and two more books and finally I got a "real job" job. A local radio station had me DJ a late night one hour poetry/spoken word show. When I first went on the air I was almost 29.

I am now 37. I am still doing the radio show and in total I have 6 books. Between the books, radio show and the odd performance or freelance gig I am able to live comfortably in a small house in a trendy area of the city. I will be paying off the house for another 10 years or so. The mortgage, job(s) make me feel as normal as I ever will I guess. It seems to me that living in and around "normal" you start to think that you are "normal" even if you aren't. Besides all of this and that I can come and go when I please. I even get 2 weeks holidays from the radio station. I mainly use the break to re-acquaint myself with my parents. The relationship between my parents and myself though is still strained.

I have had friends and I have had lovers, not many of either though. I know this is jumbled up and mixed up at times but this is me and this is dated and I will move on to the main presentation of my "auto-biography", diary, dialogue, whatever. I would like to believe that this is jumbled up because of the following incident in the cafe I am in. Or hopefully it is not me losing any of my "talents". In the cafe my brain was jumbled up and that's how I will begin...eventually.

### *-for every animal you don't eat, I will eat three-*

Obviously I've left out some parts of the beginning of my entry. Like, what was my childhood like, did I have many girlfriends or friends, how did I do in school, at home, etc, etc., etc.. All of this is unimportant now. You will find out most of it by the end, so there is no point in this line of questioning right now. Now is the time to begin this "tale".

I had just finished my radio show and on my way home I made a small, but regular, detour to a cafe (I hate that word, it just sounds so pretentious, anyways...) that's open 24 hours. It is quiet and dark and has lots of little nooks and crannies where I can hide from society. It seems somewhat trendy at certain times within the 24 hour period. Fortunately the trendy times do not usually come after my radio show, since it is a Thursday after all.

The cafe is called "Carmen's" and you enter through one door into a waiting area, almost like you are to wait to be seated. Then another door, I call this small area "the cattle room" because if it gets busy then people get crammed in there trying to leave or wait for a seat. Going through the second door your eyes adjust to the darkness and you see dark carpeting, dark wooden panels separating each booth, almost like a lounge/bar. The booths seat four people comfortably or six if you are one big happy family. The booths cover three of the four walls. Then there are about twelve tables that each seat four. The wall at the back is behind a "bar" where you order your food and coffee. There is an entrance/exit for the staff and a typical serving area at the opposite end of the staff entrance/exit where you get your meal. The long bar has a few stools and hides all the gadgetry that they have in cafes. I don't know what any of this is because I don't drink coffee or anything with caffeine in it for that fact. Most of the staff are familiar with me because I usually order a milk or juice with a chef's salad and a sandwich. As for the bathrooms, where my "meeting" happened (more on this later), they are opposite the customer entrance/exit in a corner and down a hallways a bit.

I usually seat myself in a corner booth on the same wall as the customer entrance, so I can see who enters but they can't see me until their eyes adjust from the "light" in the "cattle room". This time is no exception, "my" booth is free, so I greet the staff, ask for a cranberry juice and get myself settled in for another uneventful but relaxing evening.

Now you should know by now that when a writer says, "settle in for another uneventful but relaxing evening," that the evening is going to be just the opposite. That is exactly how mine was, or at least it seemed that way to me. I will have to set you up a bit by telling you how I "act" in the presence of other people.

In this quiet cafe I sort of notice people, I say sort of because I am usually in my own little world, and as long as no one pisses in my ocean, I don't come out of it. I do sometimes notice people though. It is like I watch people sometimes to see how they react to each other, what they say, look like, wear and so on and so forth.

The evening overall, <u>was</u> uneventful, so I will skip over some of the details. I noticed someone enter as the cafe started to get a little busy. She was a very petite blonde woman in her mid to late twenties and I found her very attractive. So I did what I always do when I see an attractive woman: I leave my table and go to the washroom. Not to do anything sick I might add, just to hide for a little while. I am very nervous around women in general, but when it comes to women I find attractive, I think fearful is the proper word.

This is usually in the beginning from the first time I see the woman to the third or fourth time I talk to her. Then I stop with the nervous laughter and the nervous little jokes. I used to think that I would get used to the opposite sex but it never worked out that way. Now I am a 37 year old stuck in the middle of puberty.

Anyways, I finish up in the washroom and come out and in the cramped hallway I run into her. Just my luck. I nervously ask her, "How about that Dow Jones?"

She snickers and smiles the most beautiful smile, nervous smile I think, that I have seen in years and then she goes into the ladies washroom, and I go back to my table and see my juice and notebook waiting for me. Even though I have been here several times, it now feels just the opposite, so I write this:

### *"I AM"*

I write this
After the first time
I meet you
I met you
I met you
In a dark cafe
That I've been to
Once or twice in my life
(It seems that way anyways)
I sit in a corner

Think to myself
Thinking to myself
And I hear a familiar melody
Go through my head
And wonder when
The last time I heard it was
And that's when you walk in
And that's when I
Thank my lucky stars
That I am not making this up
It all starts with a smile
And ends with a conversation
I wish I could write about you
The way real poets do
It's more flattering that way
I wish I could write about you
The way Goethe or Cohen
Would if they met you
For the first time
If they felt the same way
I feel about you
I wish I could write about you
The way real poets
Of past or present do
It's much more flattering
Than anything I can do
Or that's how I feel anyways
I feel like
You have the same effect on me
As does a certain song by Kronos Quartet
A passing mood that
Breezes right by and through you
Leaving you feeling
Refreshed and with a clean head
I really wish
I could talk about your eyes
Or your golden hair
The way real poets do
But I am still a half poet
Who every once in awhile
Has his peace pleasantly disturbed
By someone like you or

> By my writings
> What else can I say but
> I hope that I will meet you again
> I hope that we will meet again
> And we can talk further
> Freely again
> Not having to worry about
> Offending each other
> Because it's just talk
> Because it's just opinions
> And neither are meant to hurt
> I wrote this
> After the first time
> I met you
> I met you

---

Damn! I am so melodramatic and hopeful too, a conversation, yeah right! Oh well. The blonde "Dow Jones" woman comes out and smiles at me and goes to an end of the cafe where I can't see her. Probably for the better anyways. "Anyways," my favorite word.

Just then Sandra comes in and waves to me. Sandra is a good friend who used to be a lover of mine but we split amicably. I think it affected me more than her. I think that Sandra would agree to that and would probably add that I need to lighten up a bit. Sandra is pregnant with another man's baby. The guy took off so we now spend almost more time together than before we broke up. Sandra has long black hair and dark brown "honest" eyes.

We see each other almost always after my radio show, Sandra knows my routine and I don't mind hanging around her. She was the first friend I made when I moved here years ago. Right now I have my co-workers and my bosses at the radio station, my lawyer, my agent, my publisher and Sandra. I am a very shy person, so this is all the people I have in my life. Most times I am okay with this because I am so busy writing that I don't have much time for people outside of my work. Sandra sits down and asks in her loud voice, "How's it going?"

"Not bad," I respond sipping on my juice thinking that I need a salad to tide me over till bed-time.

This is basically how Sandra and I met and became good

friends and briefly lovers. She noticed me before I noticed her and just sat down at my table, asking if I was new around here. She has a good sense of a person before she even knows their name, it is somewhat uncanny.

Soon with her outgoing nature she was showing me around town as a friend, then dating, then loving, then full circle and being friends again, just that we still loved each other. When we were lovers I didn't know what I really wanted and Sandra as usual picked up on that and that's why we broke up. Again I am a poet, not a biographer, let alone an auto-biographer so I apologize for the bouncing back and forth. I hope to get better at this before it ends because you never know, my publisher may want an auto-biography.

Sandra compliments me on my show and I ask how the oven is cooking and so on and so forth.

"You're a little distracted tonight," Sandra blurts out.

"I just...ran into a woman and I made a fool of myself, I was nervous."

"You are too hard on yourself and I think that it is cute that you are so worried about the impressions you make on women. I mean you were fine with me weren't you?"

"I was still nervous."

"And you said to me that, I made you relax. You just need to find another lady who will help you relax. Sooner or later she will come along and then you'll write another book about it, and make more money off of our backs." Sandra smiles her wide smile and I know that she is good to have around and that she is right about me.

Sandra continues, "If you saw her here, you'll see her here again and if it doesn't work out don't let it get you down, eventually you'll find someone. I've got a few months before my someone comes along," she says as she pats her tummy and then kisses my right hand.

### *-I don't brake for goth chicks-*

I haven't really explained my radio show, so I now will. My show is on an independent/community station from 10pm to 11pm, on thursdays. I have divided it into three 20 minute sections. One section is of classic poets like Homer to Poe to Emily Dickenson. Another section is for more modern writers like

Bukowski and Cohen. The final is for new or up and comers, mostly stuff that has been mailed into me.

Some nights I will start with new, then classic and then modern and then new. Other nights I will mix it up and start with classic, then modern and finally the new material. I accept tapes, cds, etc. and I will play almost anything, within reason. I want to keep my job so if it has excessive swearing, etc. I probably won't play it. I get almost 40 different submissions a week. Sometimes a little more and sometimes a lot less. The station trusts my opinion since I have had 6 books published which sell reasonably well. Sometimes I even write articles for the local weekly for some extra cash. With the radio show, my books and the odd freelance job, I make a modest living. The station and my publisher are very supportive, so you could say that I am comfortable.

One might wonder why I look for a lover , for I seem content. Including Sandra I have had three lovers. Blood still pumps through my veins and I am still lonely at times. I am not looking for a muse, my work is my muse. I think it is insulting towards your lover if she or he is just a muse. That's my story and I am sticking to it, thank you very much. Now for my favorite word, anyways...

### *-there are very few nice bus drivers, so I call the nice ones, mercenaries-*

Before I got the radio show 8 years ago I always felt like the odd man out all of the time. This feeling started way back in junior high school. The cliche, "I was the last one picked in sports" applied. Then later on, getting fired from good or bad jobs or the worst was getting laid off from a job I really liked. Just when I would get a good paying/good work job in my grasp it would be pulled away.

Even in relationships I felt this way. My first two girlfriends dumped me saying things like I was "too sensitive" or "too emotional" or "too affectionate" or too this or too that. And then it was over. I missed almost the same things in a good job that I did in a relationship. The bonding, friendship, etc.. Depression would set in and I would be knocked down for weeks, sometimes months. It seemed like nothing ever worked out.

Somehow my writing kept me going and an agent finally accepted me and she was aggressive. Within months of losing my last job and the break up with Sandra I had a publishing contract. That was about 11 years ago.

Sandra popped in my life right when I moved here. She saw me writing at Carmen's a few times and just came up and sat down with me. I liked her forwardness, it took pressure off of me. We went out for about a year and a half and then we felt we would make better friends than friends and lovers. The reason for the break up was I got so into my work that I would put her on the back burner. She would flirt with other guys and we wouldn't see each other for weeks on end. Eventually we both broke it off and became best friends and I pitched my radio show idea to the station. They liked it and I had a job. At the time of getting the show I had already had 2 books of poetry published. They were both runner up for some awards and got good reviews. I am quite sure this helped me get the radio show.

And as cliche as it sounds, the rest is history. I am in Carmen's right now writing this down when I see the blonde again, going to the washroom, she sees me, smiles and nods and I wave. Most of this will probably be written in Carmen's because I have felt the need to get out of my house. The ulterior motive is to see the blonde girl again. Now I have seen her again and it went okay.

She goes and sits with 2 females, nods to me and continues conversing with her friends. That's enough "flirting" for today. I finish my salad and juice and get up to leave, on my way out I wave to her, she smiles and melts my heart. I leave knowing that I will see her again and I hope that I am not getting ahead of myself by asking myself, "is she the one?" How mushy is that?

## -honk if you hate people-

Maybe I am not good at sports or card or board games but I know that I am a respectable writer. I also know a lot about books and music and a little art mixed in for good measure. I thought that I would write this down before my show because I might forget it.

Like I said before, I have a feeling that this might be mostly written in Carmen's because I have got to get out of my house more often and maybe I would see the blonde lady again (the ulterior motive again). Sandra made these two points at our last meeting and I agreed. I sort of made a promise to her and myself.

Kronos Quartet's "Water Wheel" is starting, so I have got to go, but there will be more. Again, probably at Carmen's.

### *-honk if you ate people-*

Sometimes I read people's poetry on air, it is hard because I am never sure how the poet reads it. With someone like Evelyn Lau I've heard her read so I have a rough idea. But someone that I don't know...that's tough, but I do my best.

Tonight's show was pretty good, the new stuff was solid and I picked some classic like Dylan Thomas and Robert Frost. I even chose a Bob Dylan song (since I had some Dylan Thomas). I guess I should stop bragging.

I have this problem with women. I don't know when to shake hands, when to hug, when to kiss or when to walk away. I get the jitters so bad I sometimes wonder if I need pills for that. Growing up I never had one girlfriend, I had friends who were girls but nothing intimate. I was always interested in the arts. Girls sometimes flirted with me but I was never sure how to read them. So I drifted inward and could hardly wait to move and to see bigger and brighter things. My parents kind of hoped I would stay home and take over the farm. They resigned themselves to the fact I wouldn't because I was always absorbing as much as I could about Vancouver, Toronto and Montreal. From a very young age I always dreamt of getting lost in my art in a city, it didn't matter if it was Calgary or Winnipeg or larger, just work on and perfect my craft. I will say it again and this will be the last time, it does <u>not</u> matter what city I am in. Just that I am writing and I can get lost and I am now finally in my element.

Carmen's has become my home away from home when I am writing this. Besides the poem at the beginning, I have been writing my poetry at home and this, my "autobiography" here at Carmen's.

Suddenly I feel someone standing over me. I look up and meekly say, "hello," because it is the blonde standing over me smiling.

### *-if "J. Lo" had half a brain she would shoot herself and put her out of our misery-*

"You come here a lot, don't you?" she asks. Before I can answer she says, "I've seen you here several times before the 'Dow Jones' in the bathroom hallway."

I stand up with my hand out stretched and I tell her, "I am Wayne Milton. It is a pleasure to meet you. You are?"

"Daphne Scott, pleasure to meet you too. Am I interrupting anything?"

I tell her no and to sit down and that it is just a little homework and it will probably end up in my most useful tool, the waste basket. She laughs at this and her green eyes light up as well as the rest of her face.

"Is this what you do for a living?" asks Daphne.

"More or less. I have a radio show, a publishing contract and I do a little freelance and that's about it. How about you?"

"Nothing as exciting, a bank teller but it pays the bills and gives me time to..."

"Hey folks!" says Sandra. She surprises the two of us almost as if you had been dozing for about 20 minutes and the phone rings to pull you out of your slumber.

I stand up and do introductions while Sandra has a smirk on her face. I know what that smirk is about. Sandra thinks that it is cute when I see other women because I get all nervous like a junior high school student.

Daphne asks Sandra when she is due and Sandra tells her 4 weeks. I notice no tension between the two.

"Good show Wayne, I liked the way you read the Dylan Thomas piece."

"Your show was just on?" asks Daphne.

I tell her I got off the air about an hour ago. Daphne asks for the station, day and time and seems to make a mental note. Then she asks if that's why she has seen Sandra and I here at this day and time a few times before.

"Wayne and I go way back," states Sandra, "We met about 9 or 10 years ago around the time Wayne first moved here."

"Where did you move from?" Daphne asks me.

I tell her the town in Manitoba that she doesn't recognize and then explain that I lived in several cities off and on for 8 or 9 years.

"He's seen more of Canada in 3 months than I have in 3 years," blurts out Sandra.

"Wow, I have only lived here," Daphne explains.

"I didn't know where I fit in," I shrug my shoulders and say, "Now I do."

Sandra excuses herself saying she is going to the ladies room.

"Are you two..." Daphne starts.

"Lovers?" I finish, "No, we tried that and it didn't work out." I continue, "I am not the father either."

She is silent for a bit and I wonder if this has satisfied her curiosity. I am about to make a joke to break the silence when she asks if I am going to be here Saturday, same time, same place. I tell Daphne that I could be if she wanted me to be. She says yes and gets up like she is going to leave. I get up too and she hugs me gently telling me to say good bye to Sandra for her and that she will see me Saturday. As she leaves I watch her go.

Suddenly there are fingers snapping in front of my nose and Sandra saying, "Wakey! Wakey!"

I apologize and she asks if the two of us are going to meet again. I tell her yes and it will be soon. "Keep me apprised colonel!" Sandra says while tousling my hair with her right hand. "I think that it's cute!" She tousles my hair again.

I tell Sandra half heartedly to stop it and she does. I ask her if the countdown has begun, because she goes on maternity leave in 2 weeks from her job as a librarian at the main library downtown.

"You know it!" she shouts and gives me two thumbs up. We chat for a couple of hours about this and that and then go our separated ways. Me with a combination of a bit of a buzz and a bit of a worry on about Saturday.

### *-Nazis are biodegradable-*

Friday morning I am having toast and jam and at exactly 11:30 am I make a promise to myself, it is to <u>not</u> to think about Daphne and/or Saturday. At exactly 12:14 pm I break my promise. Good thing I cut caffeine out of my diet or I would really be wired. And it's not even Saturday!

Last night was horrible. I just tossed and turned in bed, wondering several times if Daphne did the same. I can't see it. She seemed a little nervous but only when Sandra was around. Most women see me as a troubled younger brother. I hope that that doesn't happen this time.

Things like this always seem like they are going so fast, except for the build up for the date or the like. I should probably explain a little better. Whenever a relationship (new lover) has just started or just finished it seems like time has flown by. But when I am waiting at dating's doorstep time crawls at a snail's pace. I think that's a better way of explaining it?

Also, I am always afraid of jinxing the whole thing. I am not very superstitious, but when I think something like, "I can almost taste it," "it" almost never works out. When I say "it" I mean the whole "kit and kaboodle," relationship, thing...

I have no freelance jobs to delve into and very few new pieces by other poets to go over and I just can't write anything except for this. I put on the stereo some *John Lee Hooker* to calm me down and I go and lay on the couch in my housecoat and underwear and I realize that I am drifting into sleep....

### *-how about a nice big cup of shut the fuck up-*

I wake up and the stereo is silent and the clock stares at me silently showing the time of 4:36 pm. Supper time and I am not very hungry, but I know I should eat something or my stomach will get worse. We didn't even exchange phone numbers! What if she gets sick or changes her mind?!

I get dressed and make toasted tomato sandwiches watch some television. I decide that I will have a long hot shower to relax and then try to read a little. I pick something that should be light and that I haven't read already, *"Concrete Island"* by *J. G Ballard.*

The shower was great, didn't do too much thinking. I start reading in bed and at first I get to page 36 and have to start over at page 28 because I lost my train of thought. Last thing I remember is looking at the page number 54 and then drifting off to sleep....

### -i'll put my foot so far up your ass i'll knock your teeth out-

Sometimes when I get so worked up (usually it is about the opposite sex or mistakes at work) I wander around the house for awhile and when I (eventually) go to bed I can sleep for hours. Last night and this morning are just such a time for it is almost 1 pm and I have decided to go to Carmen's for supper and have my usual juice and Chef's salad. As for the four hours in between I decide to make a fried egg sandwich and go over some of the mail from the station until I go to Carmen's. I live in a fairly trendy area of the city and Carmen's is within walking distance.

Going over the mail I realize it is slim pickings. More of the same old, "Man scorning cunt woman," and, "Scorned woman being angry at man scorning scorned woman." I will have to get to the station on Monday <u>and</u> Tuesday <u>and</u> Wednesday to see if there is something more unique than this trite material. It only happens once in awhile (and I am glad about that because it means more stress) a last minute radio show. Oh well, nobody and nothing is perfect.

I look at the clock and it is almost 6:30 pm and I am hungry again. I can't believe that time flew by the way it did!

Walking over to Carmen's I am going to break a promise that I made to myself when I started this "autobiography," which is talking about the weather. It is a beautiful fall day, the trees are all orange and yellow and it is warm enough that you don't need a jacket but cool enough that you should wear a sweater. The sun is bright and there are only a few small clouds in the sky.

I get to Carmen's and order my food and chit chat with the staff and such. I find that my usual table is taken so I have to sit half way between the "cattle room" and the "bar." I can watch for Daphne because the windows are fairly close to me. My food comes and I wonder why I haven't been infatuated with any of the female workers at Carmen's. Some of them are cute and pleasant to deal with. Maybe subconsciously I don't want to screw up and not be able to come back here again. Then I wonder why I always fall in love in the summer/fall and almost always break up before Valentine's day. Maybe I don't want to be burdened by such a silly pressure filled so-called "romantic" day...I don't know? I decide to write some poetry about these topics for a new book because it has been almost 2 years since my last one and I know for sure that my agent and publisher will be asking for one soon.

### *"BIGOT POEM?"*

Someone I know
Asked me why

> I don't like China or Korea
> My answer was simple
> They are always bullying Japan
> Korea kidnapped Japanese children
> And used them for who knows what
> And as for China
> Look no further than their human rights violations
> Tianemen Square and their brutality towards Tibet
> I have always gone for the underdog
> And Japan is just that
> As well as having a beautiful culture
> They have beautiful people
> The repression in China and Korea
> Shows on the faces
> Of each member of those two (three?) countries
> Unless the members escaped
> To a better place
> So if I sound like a bigot
> Too bad
> And I will never be able to hug
> Every Japanese citizen
> And that is too bad too

---

Wow! That came out of nowhere. Sometimes I feel like I should keep some things to myself, but this may raise eyebrows and luckily my publisher likes the "controversial." My gut says they may bounce it but I have written harsher that's been accepted, but borderline bigotry...I don't know.

"Hey Wayne," it's Daphne, "am I interrupting again?"

"No, that's okay, I have done enough writing for today. Please sit down."

She smiles and I finally notice her other attributes. She could be a model if she wasn't so short. Basically everything looks good to me. She's wearing a brown baggy wool sweater with a giant white petalled flower, with a yellow middle. The flower is taking up the whole front of the sweater. I almost can't believe she showed up and I definitely can't believe it is 10 pm already!

Silence.

I ask Daphne how her week was at the bank.

"Same old, same old. Pretty much a routine by now. How about your week?"

"A little writing for another book. More listening and reading and writing for next week's show. That's about it. I try to have a routine but it doesn't usually work out that way, but I get by."

"Sounds interesting. I can't help but think that it must have been a pretty big leap coming here from such a small town. I know it is off topic, but I was just curious..."

"It was a bit of a shock at first, but once I started writing for work I could express my shock that way. You said that you've only lived here."

Daphne explains that after University she went to Europe for a month and that's the extent of her travelling. Her parents retired 2 years ago when she was 32. Her Dad managed a lumber yard and her Mom was a nurse. She sees them every other week. Daphne took administrative accounting but she didn't like it. She is an only child too.

I tell her that I can relate, for after high school I was to take over the farm but I turned into a wandering writer for a few years. I tell her that my parents still hold a bit of a grudge because I was an only child and the farm was all set up for me. Now I see my parents at Christmas and they rent the farm to a couple down the road a bit.

We eventually relax and talk about childhood, future plans, music, books, likes and dislikes, make jokes and laugh. This goes on for about 3 hours. We discover that we have several things in common, which is a relief to me, for if we didn't it might not be meant to work out. I notice her pushing her long blonde hair behind her ears.

Silence.

"Would you like to come to my house party next weekend? It is one of my friend's 40th birthday and instead of celebrating it in her cramped apartment we decided to have a small gathering at my place. You could bring Sandra if you want?"

"Sure, should I bring anything else?"

"Just yourself is fine."

"I'll be there. Would you like to call it an evening?" I ask even though I could go on longer. She says yes and we exchange numbers and she tells me her address and to be at her place between 8 and 8:30 pm next Saturday.

Daphne and I get up and leave the low light warmth of Carmen's into the cool autumn night. We stand face to face and I don't know what to do. Surprise surprise. Before I can make a decision she hugs me and kisses me on the cheek. I can briefly smell her vanilla perfume, we let go and she says that she is looking forward to next Saturday.

"Same," is all that I can say.

As she is walking away she looks back and says that she had fun. I tell her that that's good because I did too. We wave and go our sperate ways.

Even though it is chilly out, I am still warm from her hug and kiss.

### -hot oral action-

The following Wednesday I am at the radio station sorting through what seems to be a metric tonne of mail when the secretary buzzes me, telling me someone is on line 4 for me. That is strange because I hardly ever get phone calls here.

"Hello?" I ask hesitantly.

"Wayne? It's me. Sandra. I'm calling from the library. My water broke. It's time."

"I'll be there in 5 minutes," and I hang up.

The station is downtown too, blocks away from the library in fact. I race there and pick Sandra up from the library. She looks like hell and is breathing heavily. I race her to the nearest hospital and the staff race her into a room. I think to myself that she had 2 days left before she went on maternity leave. What timing! I sit quietly in the noisy waiting room hoping that everything goes okay.

An hour and a half later a doctor invites me in to see "mother" Sandra and her baby girl. Sandra is all smiles but looks very tired cradling the baby.

"Amy," says Sandra. I caress Amy's tiny head of black hair and hug and then kiss Sandra on the cheek. I tell her congratulations and to call me when she is feeling better and we will hook up.

"Thanks for everything Wayne," says Sandra and she looks lovingly down at Amy. I blow her a kiss and leave.

### -you wouldn't know "punk" if "punk" bit you on the nose-

With all that is going on in my life right now (Sandra's new baby and the house party on Saturday at Daphne's) I decided to go home and go to bed right after my show. I was just too tired and too anti-social to go out and deal with a crowd.

I woke up around noon Friday and I was not feeling too well. The thought of not going to Daphne's house party did occur to me but that's tomorrow and tomorrow is another day. And again I didn't feel like going out, not to Carmen's or Sandra's and I don't need to go into the station until Monday. Besides that I don't even need groceries so I can hibernate. I should call Sandra to find out how Amy and her are doing. Hopefully they are released from the hospital because I just can't wait for her to call. I guess you could say that I am excited for Sandra.

I dial Sandra's number and it rings twice.

"Hi Wayne!" Sandra says in a raised voice that startles me.

"You shouldn't be allowed to have call display Sandra because I hate it when you do that." I say. Even though my number is unlisted it still reads my name off on the phone when I call.

"But you thought to call when you just woke up and see how me and Amy the poop machine are doing!" Sandra chuckles.

"I must sound tired. If you can tell I just woke up, but yes I was calling to see how you and your 'poop machine' were doing."

Sandra tells me that the two of them are doing great and that Amy hasn't cried much since she was first delivered into this world. Sandra thinks it is creepy how quiet she is.

I tell her just to wait, once Amy discovers she has vocal chords she will probably speak up. I also tell her that she was invited to Daphne's house party but under the circumstances...

"I'll take a pass. I am pretty tired and I am sure that you will take good notes," says Sandra, "You really are smitten with Daphne, aren't you?"

"I don't know yet," I respond.

"Liar, liar!" she shouts, "I can tell when you are smitten!"

"Yeah well...we'll see. I'll just say 'hi' to Daphne for you and that you just became a mother."

"Thank you. You're so cute when you are smitten," Sandra says in a baby voice.

"Thanks," I say wryly, "I'll talk to you later."

"Thanks for calling. Goodbye."

I should have known better than to lie to Sandra, she can read me like a cheap comic book. I just don't want to rush things, but I always seem to go so fast at the beginning of a relationship. I don't know if that's good or bad. Hopefully Daphne will let me know if it's going too fast or not.

    I realize that I am hungry and I quit obsessing about it for now. I make myself meatloaf and while it is cooking I have my favorite, Chef's salad. It's not as good as Carmen's but it will do. After lunch I do some writing that I end up getting so absorbed in that I didn't stop once, until about 6 pm or so because I had to go to the washroom. I am not really hungry so I go and brush my teeth and go to bed with the book *"Concrete Island"* again. This time I start from the beginning instead of guessing where I finished the other night.

    I wake up at 1:32 am with the book splayed out on my belly. It's at page 96. Again, I can't remember what I read. I wonder to myself if I will ever finish this damn book! I put it on my dresser, turn out the light and drift off into a deep slumber.

### -the more people I meet, the more I like myself-

    I wake up later on around 11:30 am and I slowly get out of bed. I have some granola and yogurt. I think to myself that I will have a lazy Saturday, then I remember Daphne's house party. Next thing you know I am starting to get nervous. At times I have been known to make myself sick over things like this.

    I look over the piece of paper with Daphne's address and phone number. I live south/east of Carmen's and Daphne lives south/west of Carmen's. She doesn't live too far from me, 22 maybe 23 blocks. I will drive instead of walking because this area on a Saturday night is not too safe to be walking alone.

    So I decide to do my laundry and while I wait I'll do some more writing. What an exciting life I lead. This all takes about 2 hours. It is pretty close to 2 pm so I decide to have a nap. I set my alarm for 5 pm so I have enough time to eat and shower and such before I leave for the party.

    I wake up at 5:26 pm to my alarm going off. Another deep sleep. Luckily I didn't wake up too late! I get up and have something to eat, shower than shave and by then it is almost 7 pm. Still a long ways off, so I get dressed in some of my better casual clothes and sit down and listen to some *Neil Young*. *"On The Beach"* is my choice, to try and calm down. By the end of the album it is a quarter to 8 and I decide to leave.

## *-if love is blind then maybe my x-ray glasses will help it-*

   I ring the doorbell at the address Daphne gave me and it is the right one because she answers the door. She is wearing black jeans and what looks to be a cotton blouse. It has orange/red flowers on it. The outfit definitely shows off her petite body.
   "Hey Wayne! You're the first one here!" Daphne says with mild surprise, or at least it sounds that way to me.
   "Well it's 8:15 so that's in between 8 and 8:30 just like you told me," I tell her. As she hugs me I recognize the vanilla smell. One thing I didn't tell her was that I waited for 20 minutes in my parked car because I came so early. She shows me into her kitchen where she has some snacks ready.
   "Wow!" I am in total shock. Looking around I see that the whole kitchen is covered with dried flowers of all types. Some are hanging upside down, some aren't..
   "Oh yeah, these...they are all from guys who buy me flowers. I can't bear to throw them out," she explains. Good thing I forgot about flowers. It looks like they would've ended up in this graveyard of sorts. I was also going to get her a bottle of wine but I don't drink so I don't know what's good or what's bad.
   She places some more crackers and cheese on the table where a large candle is burning. Daphne turns to me and comes up real close and says, "Thanks for coming. I wasn't sure if you were going to show or not, but where's Sandra?"
   "On Wednesday she gave birth to a healthy baby girl named Amy," I respond, "She says 'hi' though."
   "I can understand why she didn't come along, tell her I say 'hi' back and congratulations as well."
   I ask her why she thought I wouldn't show, but before she answers she places her hands on my hips and kisses me full on the mouth. Her mouth is open enough that I can taste apricots on her and there's that vanilla smell again. Just then the doorbell rings and Daphne walks slowly to the front door. Her head is turned to look at me and she says walking away, "Because you looked scared silly when I asked you." She snickers and says, "It was cute."
   "Jesus," I think to myself, "I am always cute. Why can't I

be handsome or something? I guess it's better than being ugly..." I chuckle to myself and shake my head.

Right then two men and a woman enter the kitchen where I have been silently thinking and munching on a cracker. They brought the wine. I am quickly introduced to the three people by Daphne and I am told that it is the woman's birthday before the doorbell rings again.

After that it is all a blur because I am introduced to about 15, 16 more people in the living room. Some know about me and some don't. For awhile it gets a little hectic so I go into the kitchen for a breather and I see the "birthday girl" and Daphne are speaking. I have a glass of water and a couple more crackers when I feel hands on my hips. It is Daphne and her face is flushed red hot.

"What's wrong?" I ask her with mild concern.

"Oh...my face? That's what happens when I have had a few." Daphne explains.

"I was looking for you because I was going to leave soon," I look at the clock that is peeking between some dried roses and it says almost midnight.

"That's a shame, but if you have to..."

She kisses me again on the mouth and I can taste the wine this time.

"Maybe you can call me sometime over the next few days and I can make you dinner or something," I ask nervously.

"Sounds good," she says quietly and walks me to the front door, "I'll talk to you soon."

"Thanks for everything Daphne," I say. As I walk down the front steps, she watches me and waves as I walk away. I can't help but smile because overall it was a good evening.

### -next time we talk you'd better be wearing a diaper-

I floated until my show the following week thinking how nice Daphne's friends were and especially how nice Daphne was. Maybe it's too fast but I am always second guessing myself. Anyways...the show goes well and after I decide to go to Carmen's and do some writing, maybe see Sandra and give her my gift.

When I enter, to my right I see Sandra cradling a sleeping Amy and Daphne crooning over baby Amy. It is a pleasant surprise to say the least. So much for writing.

"Hello ladies," I say.

"Hi Wayne!" Sandra and Daphne say in unison.

I am glad to see that the two of them get along. It could get messy if it was the opposite.

"Good thing it is non-smoking in here or I suppose you wouldn't have brought Amy in." I hand her an envelope. "Here's a gift certificate to that baby clothing shop a few blocks away."

"Why thank you Mr. Milton, it will definitely come in handy. Will you join us?" Sandra asks.

I am glad that neither of them are smokers or that would be a problem with me and Carmen's (because it is non-smoking) and especially a growing baby's health.

We all chat about my show and a little about Amy before Sandra decides to call it an evening. She looks tired and Amy has had a head start on sleeping over Sandra. Daphne and I thank Sandra for coming out and bringing Amy as well. It was good to see her again, I missed her. I tell Sandra that I will call her next week and with that Sandra bows and takes her leave.

"Hello again," says Daphne.

"Hey Daphne...thank you for inviting me to your party last weekend. I really had fun."

"Good I am glad that you came," she leans over and kisses me on the cheek and continues, "When are you going to let me see your place?"

I am beginning to like her honesty. It reminds me of Sandra a bit. A little more aggressive though, not that I mind it. I think a moment. I did make an offer at her place last weekend.

"How about a week from this Saturday?" I ask, "I have a writing gig that's due Monday afternoon that I'd like to concentrate on."

"What will I do with my time?" she asks melodramatically, "Whatever will I do with my time?"

"You're smart, I am sure that you will find something to do," I respond smiling.

We chat for about an hour more about music and our other interests. Besides, where we grew up we discover that we have a fair bit in common. She asks me what I have been up to and I tell her that I have been mainly listening to *Neil Young* because he is coming to town (this was just announced yesterday) and writing for my food and bills and mortgage. Daphne likes *Neil Young* too, so I tell her that I was listening to *"On The*

*Beach."* We agree that that is one of his better albums.
    I start to yawn and we agree that it is time to go. Daphne and I get outside and she kisses me on the lips. We embrace and there is that vanilla smell and apricot taste that I like. I tell her that I will call her and she says good and then we go our separate ways. It is very quiet now.

### -a non-smoking tobacconist shop-

    The next day I go into the station because I forgot my laptop there. When I get to my desk there is an envelope taped to it with my name on it. It is from the program director. I open it and inside there are two tickets to *Neil Young*. I run into the program director's office and thank him profusely. He tells me to calm down and you're welcome and now get out of his office before I make a mess. As I leave I can see a big grin on his face.
    I get home and ask Sandra if she would like to see *Neil Young* on his *"Greendale"* tour.
    "I'd like to but I've got Amy to look after and you've got Daphne to look after," Sandra says in a baby voice, "thanks for the offer though."
    "You really wouldn't mind if I went with Daphne?" I ask.
    "Hell no! She's your special friend. Go with her. If she won't then I will consider getting a baby sitter."
    I thank her profusely and she tells me again I am cute when I am smitten. I tell her I know in a macho/deep voice and I hang up.

### -never trust a woman who says she is on the pill-

    I call Daphne on Wednesday (I struggled not calling her earlier, but I didn't want to be a pest) when I get back home from the station and tell her answering machine to try and be at my house at 7 pm on Saturday because I have a surprise for her. As an after thought I tell her to bring her VHS copy of *"The King Of Comedy"* because I haven't seen it yet.
    Earlier I said that someone may want to publish this, but now I am not so sure. It is not an autobiography so much as it is a bunch of journal entries. It doesn't even have a real "climax!" Maybe I'll start a new style of writing, "climaxless journal entries." Then I worry about getting hurt by Daphne, which is irrational

because Sandra watches my back. She was my last lover and that ended two to two and half year ago. I nursed my wounds for about seven, eight months, but Sandra helped me through it and I now think that is why we became such good friends. So...maybe if things don't work out between Daphne and I, we'll be friends at least? Maybe we should talk about where we are going, about...about.... Just when I thought I wasn't nervous I start having a panic attack. My remedy for this is to go to bed, so I do. I just hope that I don't have any bad dreams, just dreams of the two of us getting closer.

### -doctor! there's blood in my alcohol system!-

My doorbell rings at exactly 7:21 pm (according to my stereo) on Saturday. I open the inside front door and all I see is an arm sticking up in the air holding a VHS copy of *"The King Of Comedy."* I can't help but laugh. Daphne stands up with a big smile on his face, her green eyes seem to glow. I ask if the arm would like to come in too.

"Yes it would!" Daphne says as she enters. She takes off her shoes and as she is doing this her long blonde hair surrounds her head while she is bending over.

I show her my home and she makes several compliments. We are silently standing in the living room and Daphne turns and looks me in the eyes. She stands on her tip toes and pulls my head down to hers and we kiss for what seems like hours. She starts to pull me towards my bedroom and once in she starts undressing me.

I will leave the rest to your imagination because I don't kiss and tell.

### -days like these should last forever-

Afterwards, laying in bed we talk quietly about everything and nothing, when Daphne shouts, "Hey, where's my surprise?!"

I tell her that I will be back. I return and tell her to close her eyes. Then I tell her to open them. She sees the *Neil Young* tickets in my hands and squeals with joy and asks me how I got them. I tell her that I have connections. She hugs me and pulls me back into bed. We talk a bit more and as we drift off to sleep I think to myself, what could be better than getting paid for work you love and having a beautiful and intelligent girlfriend. The cherry on top being Daphne and I going to see what maybe *Neil Young's* best tour from his best album in years, *"Greendale."* Maybe I am wrong, but boy am I lucky! Maybe the thing between Daphne and I will work out and maybe it won't, you never know until you try.

## *The End*

pages 1 through 7 of this piece
were written in august of 1994
in rossburn, mb & toronto, on
and the rest was written during 2 weeks
in may 2005 in edmonton, ab

*sorry it took so long!*

*Some of the "quotes" used are other's, some are mine
and some are a combination of the two.*

## *Thanks.*

www.ingramcontent.com/pod-product-compliance
Lightning Source LLC
Chambersburg PA
CBHW030604020526
44112CB00048B/1208